Discovering God's Unique Purpose for You

DICK PURNELL

HARVEST HOUSE PUBLISHERS

EUGENE, OREGON

Cover by Terry Dugan Design, Minneapolis, Minnesota

DISCOVERING GOD'S UNIQUE PURPOSE FOR YOU
Copyright © 2005 by Dick Purnell
Published by Harvest House Publishers
Eugene, Oregon 97402
www.harvesthousepublishers.com

ISBN 0-7369-1596-6

Printed in the United States of America.

05 06 07 08 09 10 11 12 / BP-KB / 10 9 8 7 6 5 4 3 2 1

Dedicated to our daughters:
Rachel and Ashley

We love how the Lord has fashioned you so different from each other.
Even though you were born to the same two parents,
God has designed you as individuals with wonderfully unique
qualities. We pray constantly that your faith in Christ will continue
to grow stronger and that you will trust the Heavenly Father
to fulfill His special purpose for each of you.
We are proud to be called your Mom and Dad.

Contents

Why Am I the Way I Am?

"Where am I going in life?"

"How come my life is not what I want it to be?"

"Why did You make me this way?"

Have you ever asked God those or similar questions? When you look at yourself, do you sometimes wonder about His wisdom—and maybe His love?

Have you ever tried to counsel the Lord? "If only You had made me smarter...prettier...more athletic...with a different personality...more outgoing...better organized...(and many other mores and betters)."

"I don't understand myself. I know You understand me, but why am I the way I am?"

Good questions. Who are you really? God lovingly created you unique—different than everyone else He has created. There is only one you. God doesn't make clones, and He wants to do specific, great things in your life. It all starts with His saying, "I created you to have an eternal relationship with Me. I want you to know Me in the widest and deepest way possible, using your especially designed strengths and weaknesses, talents and faults. You are a unique cluster of characteristics. Trust Me, I will teach you how to maximize your life."

Once, while sitting in a chair on a lawn high in the mountains, looking down at a vast valley spread out before me, I was impressed with the gleaming buildings and beautiful trees of the city in the distance. As I sat there looking around and taking it all in, I happened to notice a tiny ant climbing up a blade of grass near me. It would get to the top of the blade and then, with its antennae going in all different directions, try to go farther—but it couldn't.

I watched the ant descend back down the blade of grass and climb another one. From its vantage point at the top of the blade it could probably see only a short distance. And here I sat looking down at it, as well as seeing the magnificent scene of the mountains, the valley, and the city below. And I thought, *How much this is like God and me. I can see only a little bit, because my perspective is so limited—but God sees it all. His perspective is infinitely vast!*

You might say that God's perspective is "real" reality. What we see is not true, but what He sees is true. What God has done in creating you is so significant that you need to look at who you are through His eyes. Your worth as an individual is built on what God has said about you—and His perspective on you is the truth.

You may believe that your own self-perception is reality. You may want to stay in your comfort zone and do only what you think you can handle. When you focus on your weaknesses and inadequacies, you can get discouraged easily. The message of our world focuses on self-fulfillment and personal comfort. But God wants us to focus on doing His will and pleasing Him. True fulfillment comes from enthusiastically following Him and living by His truth. God has you in His heart, and you can trust His purposes to be the best for you. His desire is that you become all He wants you to be. As you trust Him for that, He will work in you to accomplish those purposes. Four different times the Bible says: "The righteous will live by faith" (Habakkuk 2:4; Romans 1:17; Galatians 3:11; Hebrews 10:38). Living by faith in God reveals His design for your life.

I remember once seeing a famous movie star being interviewed on television. As he answered a number of questions about his life, he mentioned that a psychiatrist was trying to help him because he was struggling with some personal issues. The interviewer asked an astute question, "When you walk down Broadway in New York City and see your name up there on the theater marquee in lights, what do you think about?"

The actor thoughtfully replied, "When I see my name in lights, I think to myself, *Someday, I would like to meet that man.*"

His response indicated that he knew there was a big difference between his public image (flashy, successful, rich, famous) and his private life (insecure, confused, lonely, empty). His deepest wish was to become the person the world thought he was. However, in reality he was insecure and struggling to somehow get his life in order.

Are you dealing with a similar struggle? Do you sometimes feel like you are divided into two people? The first person is the "outside you"—the one everybody talks about, says hello to, and interacts with. The other is the "inside you"—the hidden person deep down inside. This is where doubts, fears, anger, failures, and a host of other struggles reside, shut off from the outside world. Very few other people have ever seen these troubling emotions of yours. Maybe you have a hard time liking that "inside you" because you feel inadequate or self-conscious. Thus, you are afraid to reveal your inner person.

What if people discovered your "inside you"? That would be scary. Maybe you think they would disapprove of your weaknesses or reject you. The irony is that you may want someone else to know and love you intimately, but you are too fearful of rejection to risk revealing your inner you.

Do you sometimes feel like you don't even know yourself? You display a nice "outside you," but your "inside you" is a mess. Your self-esteem is beaten down, and you wonder if there is a way to get on the positive side. "Why did God make me the way I am?"

Cheer up. You are not alone. The Bible is full of people who felt the same way. Moses had painful questions about himself. In Exodus 3:4, God confronted him when he was an eighty-year-old shepherd tending sheep in the desert. Out of a burning bush, God called, "Moses! Moses!" and Moses responded by saying, "Here I am." He was shocked that God knew his name and where to find him.

But Moses had a bigger shock coming. God told him to go back to Egypt where he had grown up, and to lead His people out from the bondage they were experiencing. God promised to pour His power, wisdom, and message of deliverance into and through Moses to His people to set them free. However, Moses responded fearfully, "Who am I, that I should go to Pharaoh and bring the Israelites out of Egypt?" (Exodus 3:11).

Moses was confident in his abilities to shepherd sheep. But he felt totally insecure and inadequate to shepherd 500,000 of his own people. That was outside of his comfort zone because his self-perception couldn't see what God saw. "Who am I?" was all he could say. He considered himself inadequate and unprepared to carry out the task.

He thought he had stumped God with that plaintive response. Surely the Lord would say, "Yes, Moses, you know yourself better than I do. I am sorry I asked you to go back to Egypt to do My will. How thoughtless of Me. I will get someone more adequate for the job than you."

No. The Creator knew all about Moses and had prepared him for the task He asked him to do. Obviously, God was looking at Moses from a different point of view.

Moses discovered that the best perspective was to entrust himself to the Lord regardless of what circumstances he encountered. The God-designed Moses was the best person to lead an entire nation out of slavery. As he trusted and obeyed his Designer, Moses motivated and led his people to become a mighty army ready to conquer the Promised Land.

God wants to strengthen the deep down "inside you"! What method does He use? Not the one you've been using, to no avail. God's method doesn't focus on your inadequacies and your weaknesses but focuses on His adequacy—on all He has given you so that you can become what He wants you to be. He has laid out His method, His plan, in the Bible. Biblical thinking lines up with what God says is true, not what we say is true. Biblical thinking is the work of God, helping us to see the "big picture," which He has laid out.

Seeing yourself as your only resource is wrong thinking. Biblical thinking will help you find out what God has said about you and find His resources to help you live a life that fulfills His purposes. What pleases your Heavenly Father is for the two people in your body (the "outside you" and the "inside you") to be filled with faith in Him and His sufficiency for everything in your life.

The apostle Paul had a similar experience to Moses. He experienced a total change when the Lord interrupted his life. Here is his testimony:

> I thank Christ Jesus our Lord, who has given me strength, that he considered me faithful, appointing me to his service. Even though I was once a blasphemer and a persecutor and a violent man, I was shown mercy because I acted in ignorance and unbelief. The grace of our Lord was poured out on me abundantly, along with the faith and love that are in Christ Jesus.
>
> Here is a trustworthy saying that deserves full acceptance: Christ Jesus came into the world to save sinners—of whom I am the worst. But for that very reason I was shown mercy so that in me, the worst of sinners, Christ Jesus might display his unlimited patience as an example for those who would believe on him and receive eternal life (1 Timothy 1:12-16).

Get set for a great adventure in discovering exactly what God has said is true and what is "real reality." Find your security in what He has said and not in what your friends, parents, or the world has to say about you. In doing so, you will learn to think correctly and to live correctly. Godly living is looking at the revelation of God in the Bible, learning what God has said about you, and then putting these lessons into practice in your life.

"So then, just as you received Christ Jesus as Lord, continue to live in him, rooted and built up in him, strengthened in the faith as you were taught, and overflowing with thankfulness" (Colossians 2:6-7).

Understanding yourself is to see yourself as God sees you— nothing more and nothing less. You see your God-given abilities and resources. You utilize God's great gifts to you and trust He will guide you to fulfill His will for you.

Do you want to see improvement in your "inside you," as well as your "outside you"? Do you want to grow in your under- standing of God's will? Would you like to please God and enjoy living? Then diligently go through this 31-Day Experiment in *Dis- covering God's Unique Purpose for You.*

For one month make a significant effort to learn more about God and how to trust in Him. Take His view of you as the right view. Examine how you look at yourself and how you behave each day. In Christ you will find acceptance and fulfillment and the joy and power to live the quality of life that only He can give.

Change your attitudes so you are filled with joy and purpose, even in the middle of disappointments, problems, or failures. "For the love of Christ controls us, having concluded this, that one died for all, therefore all died; and He died for all, so that they who live might no longer live for themselves, but for Him who died and rose again on their behalf" (2 Corinthians 5:14-15 NASB).

For the next 31 days expect God to reveal His purpose for your life as you work through this experiment. That is faith in action. The Scriptures will come alive as you diligently seek to understand from God's point of view what He is like, what He has done for you, and what He thinks of you. Then integrate those truths into every aspect of your life, so that the deep-down "inside you" is strengthened and empowered. At the same time apply the Word of God to your "outside you" so that your total being reflects the love, strength, and grace of our resurrected Lord. Begin to really live out all that God has given you—not depending upon your human efforts but on His supernatural power.

Seeing Yourself as God Sees You

Take a 31-day look at what the Bible says is God's view of you. It will be revolutionary. He doesn't think like you. Even if you sat in a room for ten years and tried to figure out the meaning of your existence, you couldn't come up with God's viewpoint. His thoughts are far beyond yours. But cheer up. The Bible is God's thoughts revealed to us.

The next 31 days can be life-changing. As you do this experiment, you will begin to see beyond your limitations and humanness. You will begin to learn what God thinks and sees. Take a look at the progression of the following 31 statements. They are the titles of the days in God's Word that you will investigate. The plan is to develop a God-centered perspective of yourself. You are in for an exciting month-long journey into becoming the person God has uniquely created you to become.

Section #1—The Real You as Designed by God

1. Praise the Lord for who He is

2. Recognize who knows you best

3. The source of all our problems

4. You are totally known

5. You were created special

My Prayer

Dear Heavenly Father!

Change me from the inside out to live a life pleasing to You. As I look into myself, I find a selfish person needing desperately to know You and Your ways. I am tired of going on my independent way, trying to please myself. My deepest desire is to please You and live totally for You.

The "inside me" really needs to improve. So does the "outside me." I've got to get my whole life aligned with Your purposes. Sometimes I feel defeated or discouraged when I try to live a godly life. In fact, often I don't even understand myself. Why do I do the things I know are not in accordance with Your Word?

Almighty God, only You know me infinitely and perfectly. You made me purposefully for Your pleasure and plan. With my whole being I desire to do Your will and fulfill the purposes You have for me. Therefore, I wholeheartedly place myself into Your hands.

Saturate my mind and heart with the truth of Your Word, and guide me to become all that You want me to be. Fill me with the Holy Spirit so He will empower me to become strong inside and out. Pour into me Your love, wisdom, and courage. Build me up in Your matchless grace and goodness.

As I begin this experiment, develop in every aspect of my life the things that please You. My deepest desire is to become all that You want me to be.

Thank You for hearing my prayer. In the name of the Lord Jesus Christ. Amen!

Signed_____

Date_____

My Covenant
with God

During the 31 days of this experiment, I commit myself before God to examine what the Bible says is God's view of me and His purposes for me. Today, I make a covenant with the Lord to:

1. Spend 20 to 30 minutes each day in Bible study, prayer, and writing out my thoughts and plans.
2. Ask at least one other Christian to pray daily for me that the experiment will help me understand and apply God's plan for my life. (That person may want to do the experiment along with me so we can share together what we are learning.)
3. Attend a church each week where the Word of God is taught.

Signed_____

Date_____

Plan for Meeting Daily with God

Preparation for Each Day

1. Equipment. Obtain a translation of the Bible that you enjoy reading. If you want to use the same translation used in this book, get the New International Version (NIV). Get a pen to record in this book or in a journal your thoughts, answers to prayers, and plans.

2. Time. Choose a specific half hour each day to spend with the Lord. Pick the time of day that is best for you—when your mind is alert and your heart is most receptive to meeting with God.

3. Place. Find a particular spot where you can clear your mind of distractions and focus your full attention on God's Word. Suggestions: bedroom, office, library, living room, outdoors.

Read (10–20 Minutes)

1. Pray earnestly before you begin. Ask the Lord to teach you what He desires you to learn. Anticipate meeting with Him.

2. Read the entire passage that is the selection for the day.

3. Read it again, looking for important statements about God and His working in a believer's life.

4. Make written notes in this book under the following sections:

A and B—Study the passage thoroughly to answer the questions. Observe what God says about Himself and what He wants you to know about living a dynamic, God-centered life. As you discover more of His truth, your understanding of God's purpose for you will increase.

C—Write out your personal responses to the Scripture passages you have studied. How, specifically, are you going to apply the lessons you have learned to your life?

5. Choose a verse from today's passage that is especially meaningful to you. Copy it onto a card and read it several times during the day. Think about its meaning and impact on your life. Memorize it when you have free mental time, for example, when you are getting ready in the morning, while you are standing in line, taking a break, waiting for class to begin, going through your exercise routine, or walking somewhere.

Need (5 Minutes)

1. Pray that the Lord will give you insight into your own life.

2. Decide what your most pressing personal need is that day. It may be the same as on previous days, or it may be different.

3. Write down your request. The more specific your request, the more specific the answer will be.

4. Earnestly pray each day for God's provision of an answer. Continue to pray for the need you expressed that day and for unanswered needs from previous days. As you progress through the experiment, exercise your developing faith. Trust God to do big things in your life.

5. When the Lord meets your need, record the date and how He did it. Periodically review God's wonderful provisions, and thank Him often for His faithfulness. This will greatly increase your faith and confidence in Him.

6. At the end of the month, review all the answers to your prayers. Rejoice in God's goodness to you. Keep praying for the requests that still need answers.

Deed (5 Minutes)

1. Pray for the Lord's guidance and wisdom to help another person during the day. Try to apply the particular passage you have just studied.

2. Take the initiative to express God's wonderful love to someone. Be a servant. Behind every face there is a drama going on. Tap into at least one person's drama and share what God has been teaching you.

3. As you help a needy person, tell him or her about your faith in Christ. Here are some suggestions for helping someone:

    a. Provide a meal.

b. Take care of someone's children for an evening.

c. Help a friend study for a school test.

d. Do yard work with a neighbor.

e. Write an encouraging letter.

f. Start a Bible study.

g. Teach someone a sports activity or a mechanical skill.

h. Assist in moving household possessions.

i. Take someone out to lunch and listen to the needs expressed.

j. Fix something for a neighbor.

k. Show interest in another's interests.

l. Give an honest compliment.

m. Pray with a friend about a need.

n. Contribute money to a missions cause.

o. Visit someone in the hospital or at a retirement home.

Application

1. Write down ideas about how you can put into practice specific instructions found in the passage.

2. Devise a plan to implement your ideas.

Last Thing in the Evening

1. Read—Look at the passage again, searching for additional ways to discover God's unique purpose for you.

2. Need—Pray again for your concerns. Thank the Lord that He will answer in His way and in His time.

3. Deed—Record all that God guided you to accomplish that day.

4. Application—Look for further biblical insight to help you apply the passage to your life.

Doing This Experiment with Others

Ask a friend or a group of friends to do the experiment with you. Read in the back of this book "How to Lead a Group of People to Discover God's Unique Purpose for Them" for practical suggestions.

Pray frequently for one another that you will learn more about the Lord and how to live for Him. Encourage one another to be disciplined and faithful in completing the experiment. Share what you are learning.

My Starting Point

Before beginning this Experiment in *Discovering God's Unique Purpose for You,* take a few moments to evaluate your life. How do you feel about your relationship with the Lord? How do you feel about yourself?

In order to see measurable progress in developing your self-image, decide what you want to see accomplished in your life during the next 31 days. Specifically, how do you want God to change you? What are the most significant things you want Him to do in your life?

As you work and pray through this book, you may experience wonderful changes that come quickly. However, others may take longer—possibly a month, six months, a year, or more. It is conceivable that you'll take three steps forward in your growth and then one step backward. Don't get discouraged.

Keep moving. Progress will be made as you are faithful to do the things that God's Word reveals to you. Each small step of growth is success.

A. Something to Understand

What would you like to really comprehend about God's purpose for you? Write down your questions to pray and seek God's will about. For example:

1. What is God's will for the direction of my life?

2. How can I please the Lord?

3. What talents and gifts has He really given me?

4. How can I maximize my strengths and minimize my weaknesses?

In the next 31 days of this experiment, the most important thing I would like to understand is:

B. Something to Change

Choose one attitude or habit you would like to see changed. Here are some suggested areas to work on:

1. A bad attitude that displeases God

2. Conduct that upsets other people

3. Temptation that often defeats you

4. A habit that you know is wrong

5. Temper that is hard to control

6. A feeling of failure that discourages you

During the next month of meeting with God the most significant thing I would like to change:

C. Something to Accomplish

Write down what you would like to achieve during the next month.

1. Overcome a personality conflict with someone

2. Set a good example for someone

3. Tell a friend about Christ

4. Start a small-group Bible study

5. Develop a consistent, daily devotional time with God

6. Change a weakness into a strength

As a result of discovering God's purpose for me, I would like to accomplish:

D. Something to Conquer

Pick an area in your life that you have a difficult time dealing with. Here are some situations you may need to get victory over:

1. Feelings of rejection by someone you care for

2. Financial pressure that has you worried

3. A physical ailment that makes you fearful

4. Feelings of loneliness

5. A specific weakness that bothers you

6 Something about your looks

As I increase my awareness of God's power in me, I would like to conquer:

Discovering God's Unique Purpose for You

Section 1—The Real You as Designed by God

✿

Days 1–14

DAY
1

Praise the Lord
for Who He Is

PSALM 145:1-21

Key Verses:

The LORD is righteous in all his ways and loving toward all he has made. The LORD is near to all who call on him, to all who call on him in truth. He fulfills the desires of those who fear him; he hears their cry and saves them (Psalm 145:17-19).

Today's Focus:

What is God really like? People have many different opinions. The truth is what God has revealed about Himself in the Bible. He is worthy of praise and worship.

Read: Thank God that He has created us as unique individuals.

A. Focus on God's character. For what can you praise Him?

B. Focus on God's actions. For what can you praise Him?

C. God has affected my life tremendously. I praise Him for:

Need: Thank the Lord that He satisfies your desires in His time and His way.

My greatest need today is:

God answered my prayers today _____ (date) in this way:

Deed: Pray for opportunities to tell others about the Lord's greatness.

O God my King, I will proclaim Your works to another generation by:

*A*pplication

Write down some of the wonderful things the Lord has done in your life. Take time to praise Him for each one.

DAY 2

Recognize Who Knows You Best

GENESIS 2:1-25

Key Verse:

The LORD God formed the man from the dust of the ground and breathed into his nostrils the breath of life, and the man became a living being (Genesis 2:7).

Today's Focus:

God makes it very clear that He is the Creator of all. Everything has a purpose and function in His world. Adam and Eve, who are the parents of everyone, were given everything needed for living in God's beautiful creation.

Read: Praise the Lord God for creating the world and all people.

A. What did God give Adam?

B. What was the one thing Adam was forbidden to do?

C. Because the whole world shows God's creative power and wisdom, I will thank Him for:

Need: Pray to understand more of God's world.

My greatest need today is:

God answered my prayers today _____ (date) in this way:

Deed: Praise the Creator for His mighty works.

O Lord, let Your power and wisdom flow through me to help my loved ones and friends know how great and awesome You are. Here are some ideas that will help me do that:

*A*pplication

Read Genesis 1 and 2. What did God create each of the six days and what was His reaction to His creation? Why do you think the Lord gave Adam the job of naming all the animals? Why did the Lord create Eve?

DAY 3

The Source of All Our Problems

GENESIS 3:1-24

Key Verse:

When the woman saw that the fruit of the tree was good for food and pleasing to the eye, and also desirable for gaining wisdom, she took some and ate it. She also gave some to her husband, who was with her, and he ate it (Genesis 3:6).

Today's Focus:

God created the world and set limitations. He is the Creator, and we are created beings. All of nature obeys the Lord, but He has given us humans free will to choose to obey or to disobey. Pride is at the center of disobedience. "I will do what I want to do." That is what separated Adam and Eve from God—and each other. And we are just like them.

Read: Thank the Lord that He rules the universe and has given you free will to obey Him.

A. Why did Eve disobey and eat the fruit? Why did Adam eat the fruit?

B. What was the punishment for these who disobeyed?

Adam	Eve	Serpent (Satan)

C. I don't want to follow Adam and Eve's example. I want to obey God because:

Need: Pray for humility to admit your disobedience and sin. My greatest need today is:

God answered my prayers today _____ (date) in this way:

Deed: Pray for others who need to know the consequences of disobedience.

Dear Creator, help me communicate who you really are. I want to share Your message with:

Application

Satan will tell you several truths to make you believe one of his lies. What makes temptation so powerful is that it is attractive to us to meet our desires. Read 1 John 2:15-17 and compare the three areas of temptation described in this passage with Eve's temptation in Genesis 3:7. How are you tempted in these three areas? What can you do to fight your own specific temptations?

DAY
4

You Are Totally Known

PSALM 139: 1-12

Key Verses:

> *O LORD, you have searched me and you know me. You know when I sit and when I rise; you perceive my thoughts from afar. You discern my going out and my lying down; you are familiar with all my ways* (Psalm 139:1-3).

Today's Focus:

Nothing escapes God's view of you. He knows you totally! And the wonderful truth is that He understands everything about you and still loves you. Even if you tried, you cannot hide from His presence.

Read: Give thanks to the Lord that He knows all about you.

A. Why is it impossible for you to hide from God?

B. How can you be certain that the Spirit of God is with you?

C. I know intellectually and emotionally that God is always with me because:

Need: Thank God you are held in His hand.

My greatest need today is:

God answered my prayers today _____ (date) in this way:

Deed: Pray for God to guide you today to enjoy His presence.

List some specific people whom you want to understand how much God knows about them. Then pray, "Dear Lord, open the hearts of these people to understand":

Application

There are many passages in the Bible where God says emphatically, "I will be with you." See, for example, Joshua 1:1-9 and Isaiah 43:1-2. Write down how your life would change if you really believed that God is always with you at every moment of your life.

DAY 5

You Were Created Special

PSALM 139: 13-24

Key Verses:

> *For you created my inmost being; you knit me together in my mother's womb. I praise you because I am fearfully and wonderfully made; your works are wonderful, I know that full well* (Psalm 139:13-14).

Today's Focus:

At the moment your life started, you were in the loving heart of God. His hands formed you in your mother's womb. From the second you were conceived to the second you die, God's hand is on you. He designed you perfectly! You are important in His plan for all life.

Read: Thank the Lord that He knows all about you.

A. What specifically does God know about you?

B. What do you want God to tell you about yourself?

C. My soul responds to God with great joy because:

Need: Praise the Lord that you are precious in His sight.

My greatest need today is:

God answered my prayers today _____ (date) in this way:

Deed: Pray for God to lead you in the way everlasting.

O God, I want others to learn about Your great design for their lives. Help me to:

Application

Compose a thank-you note to the Lord. Express your gratefulness that you are unique—different from everyone else who has ever been born. Here are some ideas for things to thank Him for: your personality, your body and how it is shaped, your facial features, the way you walk, the way you laugh, your parents and childhood, the little things you like, your talents and abilities, the things He has helped you achieve. Keep lengthening your list as you progress through this book.

DAY
6

God's Covenant of Love with You

DEUTERONOMY 7:1-26

Key Verse:

Know therefore that the LORD your God is God; he is the faithful God, keeping his covenant of love to a thousand generations of those who love him and keep his commands (Deuteronomy 7:9).

Today's Focus:

The Hebrews had been enslaved for four hundred years in Egypt. Now as they looked across the Jordan River into the Promised Land, they faced an entrenched and evil enemy. They were helpless against such a mighty foe. But the Lord God is the difference maker. As they trusted Him, He promised to demonstrate His covenant of love and power with them. Because He loves you in the same way, He will demonstrate His powerful work in your life too!

Read: Praise God that He loves you and wants to do powerful things in your life.

   A. Yes, the former slaves were facing huge obstacles, but they were led by the Lord God of Israel. He promised them He would do great things for them if they trusted Him. What were the people supposed to do to receive God's blessing?

   B. When the people obeyed God, He would:

   C. When I face difficult circumstances and feel weak, I will remember that God:

Need: Thank God for His covenant of love and mighty hand in your life.

   My greatest need today is:

   God answered my prayers today _____ (date) in this way:

Deed: Pray for faithfulness to follow God's commands today—and every day.

   O, Lord, my God, You are leading me to reach out to difficult people who need to know You. Please work in me to:

*A*pplication

Make a list of the circumstances in your life in which the Lord did great things for you. Thank Him for His faithfulness in each of those situations.

DAY
7

Look at What the Lord Has Done for You

PSALM 103:1-22

❧

Key Verses:

> *Praise the LORD, O my soul; all my inmost being, praise his holy name. Praise the LORD, O my soul, and forget not all his benefits* (Psalm 103:1-2).

Today's Focus:

As you meditate on all the things the Lord has done, you will appreciate His love and kindness toward you. Thank Him from a full heart. Worship will change your focus from self-centered frailty to God-centered confidence.

Read: Praise the Lord He has compassion on you.

A. No matter what your circumstances are like, you can sing praises to the Lord for His goodness. As you read this psalm, what can you thank Him for?

B. What are the characteristics of the Lord as found in this psalm?

C. My heart overflows with praise to the Lord because:

Need: Thank God for His great works toward you.

My greatest need today is:

God answered my prayers today _____ (date) in this way:

Deed: Praise the Lord that He satisfies your desires with good things.

I want someone else to know that the Lord is:

*A*pplication

Compose a poem, song, or letter that describes the goodness of the Lord in your life and in the world. Think of someone who is discouraged, lacks confidence, or has a negative outlook on life. Write that person a note or call to share what you are learning about the Lord's love.

DAY
8

God's Great Blessings
Given to You

<small>EPHESIANS 1:1-14</small>

Key Verse:

Praise be to the God and Father of our Lord Jesus Christ, who has blessed us in the heavenly realms with every spiritual blessing in Christ (Ephesians 1:3).

Today's Focus:

God had you in His heart before time began. He loves you and gave you many supernatural gifts that no one else in the universe could give you. Because you put your faith in Christ, you have been abundantly blessed beyond your wildest imagination.

Read: Give thanks to God the Father for His amazing blessings to you.

A. You possess every spiritual blessing that God has for you. Describe the blessings God has given you. What does each of them mean to you?

B. What characteristics of God does He display by giving you all these blessings?

C. Because I possess all these "in Christ," my deepest desire is to:

Need: Pray for greater obedience and faith to put all these blessings and gifts into practice.

My greatest need today is:

My need was met by God the Father on _____ (date) in this way:

Deed: Pray that the Lord will give you an opportunity to share with someone about all the blessings one can have "in Christ."

God is so incredibly good to me. I want to talk with another person today to help him learn about these blessings. This is how I plan to do it:

*A*pplication

The phrases "in Christ" and "in Him" appear 133 times in the writings of Paul. Using Bible search sites on the Internet or a concordance, study the Scriptures for more of these phrases in the New Testament. List some of the other blessings God has given to you because you are in Him.

DAY
9

Getting God's Blessings
into Your Daily Life

EPHESIANS 1:15-23

Key Verses:

I pray also that the eyes of your heart may be enlightened in order that you may know the hope to which he has called you, the riches of his glorious inheritance in the saints, and his incomparably great power for us who believe (Ephesians 1:18-19).

Today's Focus:

God doesn't want you to sit back and just enjoy all the blessings and gifts He has given you. In fact, you cannot do that. These are activated in your life only as you trust Him to work through you. When you pray and walk with faith in Him, God unlocks these reserved heavenly gifts and floods you with His riches.

Read: Praise the Lord that He wants you to experience the fullness of all He intends for you.

A. In addition to having faith in the Lord Jesus and love for all Christians, what else can you ask the God of our Lord Jesus Christ to give you?

B. What does Christ have power over?

C. I believe in Christ with my whole heart. In my prayers I want Him to:

Need: Pray for Christ's power to fill your life.

My greatest need today is:

My need was met by Christ Jesus today _____ (date). This is what He did for me:

Deed: Pray for greater faith in the Lord and love for people.

The Lord has done so much for me. So many of my loved ones and friends need to know Him personally. I pray that Jesus will work through me to:

*A*pplication

Think of one person who needs greater faith, love, and power of God in his life. Reread the passage for today. Now repeat the prayer given in these verses and put that person's name in the appropriate places. Continue to pray this prayer until you see God working in your friend's life.

DAY 10

Why You Were Created

EPHESIANS 2:1-10

Key Verse:

> *For we are God's workmanship, created in Christ Jesus to do good works, which God prepared in advance for us to do* (Ephesians 2:10).

Today's Focus:

When you were "made alive in Christ" by God, you began a right relationship with your Creator. He created you specifically because He loves you. You have imperfect earthly parents, but you have a perfect Heavenly Father who has an eternal purpose for you. Day by day God will show you how to live according to His will for your life. It is an exciting adventure to walk daily with your Creator.

Read: Thank God He loves you and has changed you.

A. You used to be dead spiritually, but now, through Christ, you are alive. Describe how God looked at you before Christ came into your life and now.

Before Christ	Now in Christ

B. What was your part in the change and what was God's part?

C. Because God raised me up with Christ, I want to:

Need: Pray that God will continue to change you according to His will.

My greatest need today is:

God has done great things in my life, and He answered my prayers today _____ (date) by:

Deed: Ask the Lord to do many good works through you.

It is so wonderful to realize that I am God's workmanship and He has created me to do good works. This is what I am praying God will do through me today:

*A*pplication

The word *workmanship* actually means "poem." You are God's special poem, for He has done a special work in you. Write out your testimony so you can share it with others. Compose three sections: (1) what you were like without Christ in your life, (2) how you came to know Christ personally, and (3) what changes He has brought in your life. Design your testimony so you can give it in three minutes. Then ask the Lord for opportunities to share it with others.

DAY 11

God Has Given You Unique Spiritual Gifts

1 Corinthians 12:4-31

Key Verses:

> *But in fact God has arranged the parts in the body, every one of them, just as he wanted them to be. If they were all one part, where would the body be? As it is, there are many parts, but one body* (1 Corinthians 12:18-20).

Today's Focus:

The Holy Spirit has given you a unique group of spiritual gifts that no one else has. You are one of a kind. Why? So you can be a vital part of the Body of Christ. There are no unimportant parts. You are significant in God's plan.

Read: Pray to develop your spiritual gifts to the greatest possible degree.

A. What are the spiritual gifts mentioned here?

B. Each part of a body is important to the whole body. Why are you important to the Body of Christ?

C. I want to use my spiritual gifts to:

Need: Thank God for the gifts He has given you.

My greatest need today is:

God answered my prayers today _____ (date) in this way:

Deed: Pray for a concern for other believers.

Lord, today use my gifts to:

*A*pplication

Write down each of the spiritual gifts mentioned in 1 Corinthians 12. Which gifts do you have? How can you more effectively use your gifts?

DAY 12

Love—the Greatest of All Gifts

1 CORINTHIANS 13:1-13

Key Verses:

Love is patient, love is kind. It does not envy, it does not boast, it is not proud. It is not rude, it is not self-seeking, it is not easily angered, it keeps no record of wrongs. Love does not delight in evil but rejoices with the truth. It always protects, always trusts, always hopes, always perseveres (1 Corinthians 13:4-7).

Today's Focus:

There are many fine abilities and spiritual gifts you could possess. But the love God describes is the most important quality to possess.

Read: Pray for genuine love.

A. Regardless of what gifts you have or what circumstances you face, God wants you to be filled with true, godly love. List the characteristics of that love:

B. Why is biblical love the greatest thing to possess and express?

C. My response to this passage is:

Need: Thank God that His love never fails.

My greatest need today is:

God answered my prayers today _____ (date) in this way:

Deed: Pray for patience and kindness.

Dear Father, fill me with Your kind of love so that:

Application

Write down verses 4 through 7. Throughout the passage, substitute "Christ" for the word "love," and "He" for the word "it." How does this help you understand Christ's love for you? Now put your name in the passage. Do you honestly love others that way? If not, what do you want to change? List the names of people to whom you want to show the kind of love that this passage describes.

DAY
13

Build Up the Body of Christ

EPHESIANS 4:1-16

Key Verses:

> *Speaking the truth in love, we will in all things grow up into him who is the Head, that is, Christ. From him the whole body, joined and held together by every supporting ligament, grows and builds itself up in love, as each part does its work* (Ephesians 4:15-16).

Today's Focus:

Christ is the head of the body of believers. He wants each individual part to do its work well so we will all become united and mature. You are important in God's plan.

Read: Pray to develop a mature faith.

A. Which spiritual gifts are mentioned here?

B. What are the purposes of the different gifts?

C. Using what God has given me, I will:

Need: Thank God for godly leaders and servants.

My greatest need today is:

God answered my prayers today _____ (date) in this way:

Deed: Pray that you will use your gifts to build up the Body of Christ.

O Christ, I want to grow up in every aspect of my life in order to:

*A*pplication

Reread Ephesians 4:11-13. Write down each of the spiritual gifts mentioned in this passage. Evaluate which ones you have and compare them with the gift[s] you discovered on Day 11. Ask your friends or loved ones to help you discover your gifts. Begin to use and develop your gifts.

DAY 14

A Different Way of Thinking About Yourself

ROMANS 12:1-21

Key Verse

For by the grace given me I say to every one of you: Do not think of yourself more highly than you ought, but rather think of yourself with sober judgment, in accordance with the measure of faith God has given you (Romans 12:3).

Today's Focus:

Renew your mind by studying and memorizing God's eternal Word. That is the only way to have a truly biblical perspective on life. Pass your thoughts through the filter of the Bible.

Read: Pray for a clearer awareness of your spiritual gifts.

A. God has given one or more spiritual gifts to each Christian. What attitudes are important for you to have about yourself and your gifts?

B. No matter what gifts you possess, how should you treat other people?

C. My attitudes and actions need to be transformed. This is what I will change:

Need: Thank God for His good and perfect will for you.

My greatest need today is:

God answered my prayers today _____ (date) in this way:

Deed: Pray for commitment to help other people.

Lord, use my gifts to:

*A*pplication

List the spiritual gifts in Romans 12. Add the ones mentioned in 1 Corinthians 12 and Ephesians 4. Which ones do you have? What should you do with them?

Discovering God's Unique Purpose for You

Section 2—Maximizing Your Uniqueness

Days 15–31

Date _____

DAY 15

Follow the Right Leader

JOHN 10:1-30

Key Verses:

The thief comes only to steal and kill and destroy; I have come that they may have life, and have it to the full. I am the good shepherd. The good shepherd lays down his life for the sheep (John 10:10-11).

Today's Focus:

Jesus describes Himself as the Good Shepherd. He knows you. As you follow Him, your life will be full.

Read: Pray for your relationship with the Good Shepherd.

A. What does Christ do for His sheep?

B. How do His sheep respond to Him?

C. I know I am one of His sheep for the following reasons:

Need: Thank Jesus for holding you in His hand.

My greatest need today is:

God answered my prayers today _____ (date) in this way:

Deed: Pray for Christ to shepherd you.

Good Shepherd, I am listening to Your voice. Lead me to:

*A*pplication

Study about sheep on the Internet or in an encyclopedia. In what ways are you like a sheep? How do you feel about being like a sheep? What can you do to follow the Good Shepherd more closely?

DAY
16

Stop Focusing
on Your Weaknesses

EXODUS 4:1-17

Key Verse:

Now go; I will help you speak and will teach you what to say (Exodus 4:12).

Today's Focus:

It's easy to complain and feel inadequate. Instead of focusing on what you don't have or cannot do, focus on God who has given you all the resources you need. The Lord knows your weaknesses and wants to show His awesome power through you when you obey.

Read: Thank the Lord for all He has given you—your weaknesses and His resources.

A. The Lord appeared to Moses in the burning bush and commanded him to go to Egypt to lead His people out of bondage and into the Promised Land. Moses was 80 years old and a shepherd in the desert. What did Moses think about himself? How did God react?

Moses' excuses	God's responses

B. What did God do to give Moses courage?

C. I will obey God's commands because:

Need: Thank God that He wants to do great things in and through you.

My greatest need today is:

God answered my prayers today _____ (date) in this way:

Deed: Pray for courage to help needy people.

Lord, give me Your strength to:

Application

Write down the verses that help you see God's strength in your areas of weakness. Review the verses when you feel like quitting. Read Galatians 6:7-10 and 2 Corinthians 12:9-10.

DAY
17

Listen to Wisdom

Proverbs 8:1-36

Key Verses:

Choose my instruction instead of silver, knowledge rather than choice gold, for wisdom is more precious than rubies, and nothing you desire can compare with her (Proverbs 8:10-11).

Today's Focus:

The Lord's wisdom cries out, beckoning you to learn, accept it, and apply it to your life. In today's confusing, corrupt world, one of your greatest needs is to find God's truth and base your decisions and life on it. The results will be evident as you obey Him.

Read: Thank the Lord that He understands you perfectly—and everything else in the universe.

    A. Why is godly wisdom so desirable?

B. What are some characteristics of a person who is wise?

C. Instead of being concerned about obtaining wealth and possessions, I will concentrate on:

Need: Pray to find wisdom and receive favor from the Lord. My greatest need today is:

God answered my prayers today _____ (date) in this way:

Deed: Pray that you will grasp His wisdom to instruct you how to live the best life.

Dear wise and good God, help me share godly wisdom with:

*A*pplication

Write down some areas of your life in which you need wisdom. Look up the words *wisdom* and *understanding* in a Bible concordance to find out what the Lord wants you to know. Start with James 1:2-8. Ask God to give you strength to make wise choices and obey His commands.

Date _____

DAY
18

Go from a Weakling
to a Warrior

Key Verse:

*When the angel of the Lord appeared to Gideon, he said,
"The Lord is with you, mighty warrior"* (Judges 6:12).

Today's Focus:

When God is with you, He changes everything. Gideon was
a weakling, afraid of his enemies and his own people. He felt all
alone and helpless to do anything good. But the Lord changed
him into a mighty warrior. He will do the same for you.

Read: Thank the Lord for great changes He will bring into your
life.

    A. Gideon faced many powerful obstacles. Describe the
       forces against him:

Midianites	Israelites	His family	Men of the town

B. Why did the Lord reduce Gideon's army of soldiers from 32,000 to 300?

C. When I feel like giving up and quitting, I will remember the Lord is:

Need: Pray for God to give you victory regardless of the opposing forces aligned against you.

My greatest need today is:

God answered my prayers today _____ (date) in this way:

Deed: Pray for the Lord to guide you to overcome obstacles and help bring strength to people in your life.

Lord, I need Your strength and wisdom to:

*A*pplication

Gideon faced overwhelming obstacles to liberate His people from a wicked enemy. God takes ordinary people and does extraordinary things through them when they obey Him. Study other ordinary people in the Bible who trusted God to work in their lives. Here are a few people to study: Abraham, Joseph, Deborah, David, Esther, Micaiah, Mary, Martha, and Lazarus. What did God do for them?

DAY 19

Every Day Counts

Psalm 90:1-17

Key Verses:

> *Teach us to number our days aright, that we may gain a heart of wisdom. Relent, O Lord! How long will it be? Have compassion on your servants. Satisfy us in the morning with your unfailing love, that we may sing for joy and be glad all our days* (Psalm 90:12-14).

Today's Focus:

Even though you may live 70, 80, or more years, your life is short. Eternity is far longer. Live each day with an insatiable desire to understand and experience God's eternal strength and unfailing love. No matter what your situation, He will make your days full of gladness. The wise person is the one who makes the most of each day with God's perspective in mind.

Read: Thank God that He can give you gladness and wisdom every day.

A. Compare the characteristics of the Lord and you.

God	Me

B. You will face good times and tough times, joy and pain. What is the best way to handle every day?

C. Teach me, Lord, to:

Need: Pray that your life and work will be founded on His Word.

My greatest need today is:

God answered my prayers today _____ (date) in this way:

Deed: Pray that you can help someone realize God's perspective on life.

Ideas I want to convey:

*A*pplication

Find some quotes in newspapers, magazines, or from television that describe how people with worldly mindsets look at life. What is important to them? Reread Psalm 90. Write out your responses to the world's way of thinking. Share your findings with some people who have worldly attitudes. Pray to lead them to trust in the Lord.

DAY 20

Saturate Your Mind with God's Truth

PSALM 119:97-120

Key Verses:

Oh, how I love your law! I meditate on it all day long. Your commands make me wiser than my enemies, for they are ever with me. I have more insight than all my teachers, for I meditate on your statutes (Psalm 119:97-99).

Today's Focus:

You can learn about yourself from your relatives, friends, and wise people. But God's Word is a mirror to look at yourself and how you are living. Through its pages, God reveals His truth for every day and circumstance. It gives you direction and wisdom. It is invaluable to your life.

Read: Praise God that His Word is sweet to your taste—sweeter than honey.

A. Describe the psalmist's attitudes about God's Word.

B. What does the Word of God do for a person who obeys it and lives by it?

C. I want to study God's Word with greater consistency because:

Need: Pray for a greater passion and love to study the Scriptures.

My greatest need today is:

God answered my prayers today _____ (date) in this way:

Deed: Pray for others to study and live by the Bible.

O Lord, guide me to share Your Word with others today. Here are some ideas that will help me do that:

Application

Almost every one of the 176 verses in Psalm 119 has a reference to God's Word. List the synonyms that are used for the Scriptures. Reread the passage and write down the one action of the psalmist that you most want to emulate. What is your plan for doing that?

Date _____

DAY 21

Obey God and Watch Him Work

JEREMIAH 1:1-19

❧

Key Verses:

But the LORD said to me, "Do not say, 'I am only a child.' You must go to everyone I send you to and say whatever I command you. Do not be afraid of them, for I am with you and will rescue you," declares the LORD (Jeremiah 1:7-8).

Today's Focus:

Even before you were born, God designed you with a unique purpose. To love and follow Him passionately is the greatest goal. God never said that it would be easy. In fact, the more you want to stand up for God, the more people may oppose you. You may think you are unable to do what His Word says. Remember, God is with you. He will empower you to live boldly for Him in a wicked world.

Read: Praise the Sovereign Lord that He is with you and will sustain you.

A. Jeremiah was probably a teenager when the word of the Lord came to him. What excuses did he give for not obeying the Lord? How did God respond?

Jeremiah's excuse	God's response

B. What message did the Lord command Jeremiah to proclaim to the nation of Israel?

C. Dear Lord, I will obey Your Word because:

Need: Pray for courage to obey God.

My greatest need today is:

The Sovereign Lord answered my prayers today _____ (date) in this way:

Deed: Ask the Lord to use you to share His message with others.

Lord, help me to stop focusing on my weaknesses and fear. I want to be courageous for You. Empower me today to:

Application

The book of Jeremiah is all about obedience to the Sovereign Lord. The way to look at yourself is not through your own perspective, but through the eyes of God. Look at these passages and notice how you should view yourself and your circumstances: Jeremiah 9:23-24; 17:5-8; 20:11-13; 29:11-13; and 32:17-19.

DAY 22

Look at Life from Christ's Perspective

MATTHEW 5:1-16

Key Verses:

> *Blessed are those who hunger and thirst for righteousness, for they will be filled. Blessed are the merciful, for they will be shown mercy. Blessed are the pure in heart, for they will see God* (Matthew 5:6-8).

Today's Focus:

The source of personal happiness is no mystery. God blesses people who incorporate His perspectives into their attitudes and actions. These statements are called the "Beatitudes."

Read: Pray to live by the Beatitudes.

    A. Since the word *blessed* means happy, the Beatitudes can be called "The Happy-tudes." What are the characteristics of truly happy people?

B. Regardless of your circumstances, what should you do?

C. Because I want to be happy, I will:

Need: Thank God for His precious promises and blessings.
My greatest need today is:

God answered my prayers today _____ (date) in this way:

Deed: Pray that your light may shine brightly.
Lord, let my confidence in You shine forth so that:

*A*pplication

Examine yourself in light of the qualities that Christ commends. Which of these qualities are present in your life? Which do you need to improve?

DAY 23

Build a Great Future in Eternity

1 CORINTHIANS 3:1-17

Key Verses:

By the grace God has given me, I laid a foundation as an expert builder, and someone else is building on it. But each one should be careful how he builds. For no one can lay any foundation other than the one already laid, which is Jesus Christ (1 Corinthians 3:10-11).

Today's Focus:

You have time and many opportunities to build something eternally rewarding on the foundation of Christ. Only what is done for His honor will last.

Read: Pray for determination to work hard for eternal values.

A. What materials are people using to build on the foundation of Christ? What will happen to them in the future? What are the results of our actions?

B. What is the meaning of the following concepts from today's reading?

1. God's fellow worker (verse 9)

2. God's field (verse 9)

3. God's building (verse 9)

4. God's temple (verse 16)

C. My desire is to build:

Need: Thank God you are His temple.

My greatest need today is:

God answered my prayers today _____ (date) in this way:

Deed: Pray for opportunities to point others to God.

O God, help me to plant and water the seed of the Word so that:

Application

Evaluate your activities. Write down which ones are producing gold, silver, and costly stones in the sight of God. Which ones are producing wood, hay, and straw? What will you change?

DAY 24

Invest Your Life Wisely

MATTHEW 25:14-30

Key Verse:

His master replied, "Well done, good and faithful servant! You have been faithful with a few things; I will put you in charge of many things. Come and share your master's happiness!" (Matthew 25:23).

Today's Focus:

There is a little poem with great meaning: "Only one life, 'twill soon be past; only what's done for Christ will last." What we do now will have a profound result in this world—and in the one to come. The greatest goal in life is to please our Master.

Read: Pray for faithfulness.

A. Why was the master pleased with the servants who were given five and two talents?

B. Why was the master upset with the servant who was given one talent?

C. With all that God has given to me, I will:

Need: Thank God for His generosity in giving you gifts.

My greatest need today is:

God answered my prayers today _____ (date) in this way:

Deed: Pray that you may share the Master's happiness.

Master, I am Your servant. Help me to be faithful to:

*A*pplication

Review your list of talents and gifts with which God has blessed you. Ask Him to guide you to invest them wisely for His glory. Strive to be faithful.

DAY 25

Give Generously to Needy People

MATTHEW 25:31-46

Key Verse:

> *The King will reply, "I tell you the truth, whatever you did for one of the least of these brothers of mine, you did for me"* (Matthew 25:40).

Today's Focus:

When you help people in need, you are ultimately giving to Christ Himself. Such compassion will be greatly rewarded.

Read: Pray for kindness.

A. The Son of Man, the King, will someday judge all people. Describe the kind of people to whom He will give the kingdom.

B. Why is a compassionate, righteous person so blessed?

C. Instead of being selfish and self-centered, I will:

Need: Thank God for the inheritance He will give you.

My greatest need today is:

God answered my prayers today _____ (date) in this way:

Deed: Pray for compassion for people.

Lord Jesus, bring some needy person into my life today that I may:

Application

List ways you can practically be kind and compassionate to people around you who are hurting. How can you help them socially, emotionally, physically, financially, or spiritually?

DAY 26

Seek Christ's Way and Reject the World's Way

MARK 10:17-45

Key Verses:

Whoever wants to become great among you must be your servant, and whoever wants to be first must be slave of all. For even the Son of Man did not come to be served, but to serve, and to give his life as a ransom for many (Mark 10:43-45).

Today's Focus:

Jesus modeled a life of serving rather than seeking personal benefits. As His follower, you are called to do the same. Contrary to popular opinion, the way to lead is by serving others.

Read: Pray for discernment to understand Christ's words.

A. What are the characteristics of a follower of Christ?

B. Why become a servant?

C. Instead of trying to be in control, I will:

Need: Thank Christ for serving us.

My greatest need today is:

God answered my prayers today _____ (date) in this way:

Deed: Pray for the humility to serve others.

Lord, teach me to be like You and to serve others by:

*A*pplication

List the hindrances you face in genuinely serving other people. How can you conquer them to become a servant-leader?

DAY 27

Know Where to Set Your Heart

LUKE 12:13-34

Key Verses:

Do not set your heart on what you will eat or drink; do not worry about it. For the pagan world runs after all such things, and your Father knows that you need them. But seek his kingdom, and these things will be given to you as well (Luke 12:29-31).

Today's Focus:

What you treasure reveals your value system. If you spend your time accumulating things here on earth, to the exclusion of making spiritual investments, your soul will end up bankrupt. God's provisions are given to those who treasure His values.

Read: Pray for wisdom to choose godly values.

A. What was wrong with the rich man's attitude?

B. Why is it foolish to worry?

C. I will seek God's kingdom because:

Need: Thank God for meeting your needs each day.

My greatest need today is:

God answered my prayers today _____ (date) in this way:

Deed: Pray to overcome greed and worry.

Father, I desire to be a more giving person. Guide me to:

*A*pplication

Write out a plan for how you will minimize greed
and worry. Start with making a budget to handle
your finances so you can give generously to God.

DAY 28

Pay the Price to Become a Disciple

LUKE 14:15-35

Key Verse:

> *In the same way, any of you who does not give up everything he has cannot be my disciple* (Luke 14:33).

Today's Focus:

There is a high cost for following Christ. A relationship with Him is more important than anything else. To sacrifice all for Christ is a decision you will never regret.

Read: Pray for the confidence to give up everything for Christ.

A. Why do some people miss the joy of becoming disciples of Christ?

B. How can a person become His disciple?

C. My response to Christ's invitation to follow Him is:

Need: Thank Christ for His kind invitation to be His follower.

My greatest need today is:

God answered my prayers today _____ (date) in this way:

Deed: Pray for resolve to count the cost of discipleship.

Master, lead me to people that I can invite to:

*A*pplication

Divide a sheet of paper in half by drawing a vertical line down the center. On the left side put all hindrances to your becoming His disciple. On the other side write down the ways you will overcome those hindrances.

DAY 29

Decide Why You Are Alive

PHILIPPIANS 1:12-30

Key Verses:

> *I eagerly expect and hope that I will in no way be ashamed, but will have sufficient courage so that now as always Christ will be exalted in my body, whether by life or by death. For to me, to live is Christ and to die is gain* (Philippians 1:20-21).

Today's Focus:

The difficulties you face can actually advance the gospel and not impede it. The difference is your attitude.

Read: Pray that you will exalt Christ.

    A. Paul was imprisoned for many years on false charges. What was his attitude about handling difficult circumstances?

B. Even when you are facing difficult circumstances, how can you encourage others?

C. When tough times confront me, I will:

Need: Thank Christ for giving significance to your life.

My greatest need today is:

God answered my prayers today _____ (date) in this way:

Deed: Pray for the advancement of the gospel.

Lord God, give me opportunities to proclaim Christ to:

*A*pplication

What are the three most troublesome issues confronting you? Pray about them and write out a specific plan to handle each of them.

DAY
30

Determine to
Be Humble

PHILIPPIANS 2:1-11

Key Verse:

> *Your attitude should be the same as that of Christ Jesus*
> (Philippians 2:5).

Today's Focus:

If you want to develop oneness with people, you need to be humble and relate to their interests. Follow Christ, who is the greatest model of bringing people together.

Read: Pray for the same attitude of humility that Christ had.

A. How does God want you to relate with others?

B. Why is Christ's example of humility so significant?

C. Because I want to be like Christ, I will:

Need: Thank Christ that He is the Supreme Lord.

My greatest need today is:

God answered my prayers today _____ (date) in this way:

Deed: Pray to see other people's needs.

Lord Jesus Christ, help me become a servant of others in order to:

*A*pplication

List the significant people in your life: mother, father, brothers, sisters, spouse, children, close friends, boss, etc. Write out practical ideas as to how you can improve your relationships with them.

DAY
31

Live with Your Ultimate Future in Mind

REVELATION 22:1-21

Key Verses:

> *No longer will there be any curse. The throne of God and of the Lamb will be in the city, and his servants will serve him. They will see his face, and his name will be on their foreheads* (Revelation 22:3-4).

Today's Focus:

Heaven is greatly desirable. Our lives today are wonderfully affected by the reality of our eternal future!

Read: Thank God that your future is certain.

A. Describe what God has prepared for you in the future.

B. Why is God's invitation to you so wonderful?

C. Because the Spirit and the Bride say, "Come," I will:

Need: Thank God for heaven.

My greatest need today is:

God answered my prayers today _____ (date) in this way:

Deed: Pray for the faithfulness to do right.

Alpha and Omega, help me bring others into:

*A*pplication

Knowing the future that God has for you, how does that affect how you look at your life right now?

Evaluating My Progress

Now that you've completed *Discovering God's Unique Purpose for You*, it is important for you to think about what progress you have made. This will help you plan for future development.

I. Look back at the areas you chose at the beginning of the experiment under "My Starting Point." Compare your initial desires with what you have done in the past month. Under each area below, circle the number on the progress scale that represents where you are now (1 = "I have made no progress"; 5 = "I have made very significant progress").

    A. Something to Understand

        Starting Point / Goal

        1 / 2 / 3 / 4 / 5

        Explanation of the progress I have made:

    B. Something to Change

        Starting Point / Goal

        1 / 2 / 3 / 4 / 5

        Explanation of the progress I have made:

C. Something to Accomplish

Starting Point / Goal

1 / 2 / 3 / 4 / 5

Explanation of the progress I have made:

D. Something to Conquer:

Starting Point / Goal

1 / 2 / 3 / 4 / 5

Explanation of the progress I have made:

II. God has also helped me in other areas. These are things He has done in my life:

III. Here are areas that I still need to work on:

IV. My plan of action to progress in these areas is:

V. This is what I have learned about the Lord and His greatness:

Signed _____

Date _____

Improving Myself

⁓

Discovering God's unique purpose for you is a lifelong process. You won't understand all that God has for you in a month. Yet, the Lord is committed to developing you every day of your life. "Being confident of this, that he who began a good work in you will carry it on to completion until the day of Christ Jesus" (Philippians 1:6).

Continue to meet with God each day studying His Word, praying, and applying what you learn (Read, Need, Deed). Determine to grow in faith and serve Him consistently day to day. "For Christ's love compels us, because we are convinced that one died for all, and therefore all died. And he died for all, that those who live should no longer live for themselves but for him who died for them and was raised again" (2 Corinthians 5:14-15).

Here are 31 practical biblical truths for you to put into practice as you continue to become all that God wants you to be. If you study one per day, you will continue this experiment for another month.

1. Believe God that you were made in His image (Genesis 1).

2. Know you are unconditionally loved by God (John 3).

3. Realize you are fully accepted in Christ (Romans 15).

4. Believe that Christ lives within you (Galatians 2).

5. Trust God that He will never leave you (Hebrews 13).

6. Accept God's perspective of you as the right one (Isaiah 55).

7. Learn to worship the Lord through difficult times (Psalm 34).

8. Be strong and courageous (Joshua 1).

9. Keep on remembering that you serve the risen Christ (John 21).

10. Thank God for His grace to you (1 Timothy 1).

11. Work toward becoming a leader in your church (1 Timothy 3).

12. Major in the positive things about you (2 Corinthians 4).

13. Get additional education if at all possible (Ezra 7).

14. Live for godly values even if it means suffering (2 Timothy 1).

15. Keep on praying (Luke 18).

16. Give God time to work. Be patient (Philippians 1).

17. Learn to get wisdom from the Holy Spirit (1 Corinthians 2).

18. Use your strengths to build up other people (Ephesians 4).

19. Seek God's guidance through prayer and Bible study (James 1).

20. Humbly seek God's forgiveness when you sin (Psalm 51).

21. Say No! to things that pull you down (Genesis 39).

22. Serve the Lord with your whole heart (1 Samuel 13).

23. Refuse to allow tough times to discourage you (2 Corinthians 12).

24. Do all for God's glory (Colossians 3).

25. Remember you are dead to sin and alive to God (Romans 6).

26. Daily be filled with the Holy Spirit (Ephesians 5).

27. Keep developing God-like qualities (2 Peter 1).

28. Praise the Lord all the time (Psalm 100).

29. Focus on what the Lord Jesus has done for you (Isaiah 53).

30. Keep internalizing God's truth (Psalm 119).

31. Give a great shout—the Lord is the ultimate victor (Revelation 19).

My Prayer Journal

Date	Prayer Request	God's Answer

My Prayer Journal

Date	Prayer Request	God's Answer

My Prayer Journal

Date	Prayer Request	God's Answer

My Prayer Journal

Date	Prayer Request	God's Answer

My Prayer Journal

Date	Prayer Request	God's Answer

How to Lead a Group of People to Discover God's Unique Purpose for Their Lives

⟨ornament⟩

This 31-Day Experiment (*Discovering God's Unique Purpose for You*) has been used by Bible-study groups, men's groups, women's groups, families, groups preparing for a missions trip, new-believers' groups, Sunday-school classes, and entire churches.

Doing this 31-Day Experiment together as a group has lots of benefits:

1. Everyone will be studying the same passages of Scripture during a month.

2. The whole group will be united together in seeking to know and experience God's design for their lives.

3. People will share their prayer requests with others in the group. Everyone will grow in his or her faith as members pray for one another and experience God's answering their prayers.

4. Individuals will see how the Lord is working in one another's lives.

5. Members can encourage one another in their relationships with the Lord and in sharing their faith in God with other people.

Here are some guidelines to start using *Discovering God's Unique Purpose for You* with your group:

1. Remind the people of the purpose of your group—and the need to deepen their relationships with the Lord.

2. Introduce the 31-Day Experiment goal—to build a habit of spending 20 to 30 minutes each day with the Lord in Bible study, prayer, and application of God's Word to life.

3. Show how the book fits into the purpose for your group. Share ideas and passages of Scripture to build one another up. Motivate the people to seek to increase their knowledge of God's Word and to pray more fervently.

4. There are 31 days of study. Do the first day together as a group with the leader showing how to do the study. Encourage group members to all start on the same day (preferably the next day) so that each person will always be on the same experiment day. If at all possible, try to meet weekly. Therefore, when the next meeting occurs, they will have done six days of the experiment.

5. Plan to do the experiment with your group in five weeks. Each week the group members should start the experiment days on the day after the group meeting. On the day meeting, members should not do the day's

experiment. Rather, they can spend that day reviewing their notes for the previous six days and thanking the Lord for all He has done in their lives.

6. When the group settles on the day they all want to start the experiment, send an e-mail reminder of the date to each person, as well as a reminder of the time and place for each weekly meeting. Designate one e-mail address to which people can send e-mails about the things they are learning, prayer requests, and answers to their prayers. Send all the e-mails received to the whole group each day to encourage people to keep doing the experiment. This will help build group unity and spiritual growth.

7. Encourage members to use a Bible dictionary, Bible concordance, or word-study book when they need to understand passages better.

8. Encourage the group to bring their Bibles and their *Discovering God's Unique Purpose for You* books to each weekly meeting.

9. When you meet, discuss each day of the previous week's experiment consecutively. Ask people to share with the group what they learned and how it has affected their lives.

10. If your group is large, you may want to divide into smaller subgroups, preferably five to six people in each group. Ask the people in the group or smaller subgroups to call one another during the week to see how each person is doing, answer any questions, and pray

together on the phone. In this way, each person will receive several phone calls a week.

11. At the conclusion of each group meeting, pray together, praising the Lord for all He has done and asking Him for consistency to do the experiment faithfully each day. Pray that each person will look forward to meeting with the Lord daily and will experience His presence in their lives during the week.

12. Use the following as a simple format for the weekly meetings.

Weekly Group Participation Outline

Subject: Discovering God's Unique Purpose for You

Content: Review the previous six days

Tips for the Leader

1. Prepare your lesson early, asking the Holy Spirit to give you ideas on what to teach and how to draw all the members into the discussion. Be creative. Use a variety of ways to communicate, such as videos, music, drama, and objects—whatever it might take to make the lessons meaningful.

2. Start with an icebreaker as a way of getting to know one another a little better.

3. Begin with the whole group together, interacting on what they learned that week. Or if your group is large, you may want to split up into subgroups. This will allow a greater number of people to share about their experiences.

4. Find out what hindrances they encountered as they sought to meet with God each day. Discuss how to discipline yourselves to consistently spend time with the Lord in the midst of hectic schedules.

5. Let everyone give input on the first day's topic before going on to the second day's topic.

Questions for Discussion

1. How was your meeting with God each day this past week?

2. What did you have to do to set aside the 30 minutes each day?

3. What did you learn about understanding God's character? Loving God? Obeying God?

4. What answers to prayer did you receive? What are you still praying about?

5. What kinds of responses did you receive when you reached out to other people?

Closing

1. Celebrate all that God has done during the past week.

2. Discuss the week ahead and the passages you will be studying. Build interest and excitement for the new things you will encounter and learn.

3. Close in group prayer. Lead in praising the Lord for His working and in asking Him to draw everyone closer to Himself during the week.

4. Motivate the people to pray earnestly for one another during the week. Remind them to phone others and send e-mails about their experiences. Encourage each other to share their faith with people who don't know the Lord personally.

At the end of the five weeks of the experiment:

1. Conclude with a special dinner, or order pizza. Build a fun atmosphere.

2. Make the time a celebration of completing the experiment.

3. Focus attention on the Lord and how wonderful He is.

4. Share testimonies of changed lives and healed relationships.

5. Introduce another 31-Day Experiment. Plan for what you will do next to keep growing in faith and building your group fellowship.

6. Motivate the members to invite their friends to participate in the new experiment. Encourage them to pray for their friends that they might join the group and get involved in discovering God's unique purposes for their lives.

7. Encourage each person to consider starting their own *Discovering God's Unique Purpose for You* group with their friends or neighbors.

Additional 31-Day Experiment Books

Now that you have finished a month of studying God's Word and discovering your God-given purpose, I hope you will want to continue to spend time alone with the risen Lord. He is the Vine from whom you can receive daily life and nourishment. Intimacy with Him continues and increases as you daily remain in Him.

The 31-Day Experiment series has been designed to help you develop a consistent devotional time with your Heavenly Father. Whether you are a new Christian or have been one for a long time, these 31-Day Experiments will help you establish an intimate relationship with Christ. You will experience for yourself the joy of discovering God's truth from the Bible.

All the Experiment books are designed like the one you have just completed. Each book focuses on a different theme in the Bible and includes relevant passages for you to study.

At the end of each experiment you'll find a number of simple Bible study methods or ideas for further growth. These will help you investigate, on your own, more of the truth that the Holy Spirit wants to teach you.

These books are designed to help you get into God's Word and get God's Word into you.

Growing Closer to God

This 31-Day Experiment book will help you increase your knowledge of God by having you look at passages in which you can discover more about His ways and perspectives. The process of continuing to know God intimately will affect every area of your life and actually will begin to transform you into the kind of person He wants you to be. Some topics in the book are:

- God's Plan to Provide for My Needs

- Assurance of Eternal Life

- Peace with God

- Experiencing the Power of God

- Living with New Purpose

- Guidance from God

- Living by the Spirit

Three additional Bible study methods are also explained. The first is a "One-a-Day Bible Topics." You will learn how to find out all that God says on any biblical subject that interests you.

The second is "One-a-Day Scripture Meditations" that will show you how to get the most from focusing on a passage of Scripture.

The third is "Big Lessons from Little People" in which you will investigate the lives of biblical people. To start you off, 15 people are suggested. Each one can be studied in 30 to 45 minutes. The Holy Spirit can teach you some vital lessons through these ordinary individuals.

Knowing God by His Names

This book took me 13 years to write. I first became interested in the fascinating variety of the names of God when I was a pastor in Indiana.

I started a search in the Bible for God's names. A name to the people in biblical times meant something entirely different from what it does to us today. In our culture a name is given to a child to identify him or her from other people. But a name in the Bible refers to a particular trait or characteristic about the person. If you understand the meaning of his/her name, you will know something very important about him/her.

Our great Lord has over 200 names! God has so many names because each one puts the spotlight on a particular aspect of His infinite, rich character. No one name could tell you everything there is to know about Him.

This experiment gives you a different name to study each day. By learning about each name, your understanding of God will increase, and your love for our wonderful Lord will grow deeper.

Here are some of the names you will study during the 31 days:

- Father

- LORD (Jehovah-Sabaoth) Almighty

- Prince of Peace

- LORD (Jehovah)

- Most High God

- Living God

- LORD (Jehovah-Rophe) Who Heals

- Son of Man

- Counselor

- King of Kings

Your prayer life will be transformed. When you have a specific need, you will be able to address God using the name that deals with that situation.

- **Anxious?** Lean on the Prince of Peace.

- **Hurt?** Experience comfort from the Heavenly Father.

- **Guilty?** Find forgiveness from the Lamb of God.

- **Insecure and fearful?** Look to the Rock.

- **Looking for direction?** Follow the Shepherd.

- **Confused?** Come to the Light of the World.

In the back of the book, you will find a list of more than 200 names for God, their characteristics, and a key verse to get you started in learning about each name. In addition, there are practical directions to help you unlock the mysteries of God's divine Person.

It is an exciting approach to developing intimacy with the Lord of Glory. He wants to reveal Himself to you so that you will respond in obedience, faith, love, and worship.

About the Author
Dick Purnell

Dick Purnell is an internationally known speaker and author. He has spoken in all fifty states in the United States as well as in twelve other countries. He is the Executive Director of Single Life Resources, a division of Campus Crusade for Christ. Dick and his wife, Paula, are on the national speakers' team for FamilyLife Marriage Conferences.

He has authored thirteen books, including his latest, *Finding a Lasting Love*. Some of his other books are: *Free to Love Again, Building a Strong Family, Making a Good Marriage Even Better, Growing Closer to God* and *Knowing God by His Names*.

A graduate of Wheaton College, Dick holds a master of divinity degree from Trinity International University, as well as a master's in education, specializing in counseling, from Indiana University. He is an adjunct professor at New Life Bible College in Moscow, Russia.

Dick has been featured on many national television shows, including *The Coral Ridge Hour*, *The 700 Club*, and *The Nashville Hour*. He has been the main guest on many radio programs, such as *FamilyLife Today*, *Moody Broadcasting*, *Truths That Transform* and *America's Family Counselors*.

Bring Dick Purnell to Your Area

Dick Purnell speaks to audiences throughout the United States, Canada, and in many other countries. For information about the wide variety of topics he presents, contact him at:

Dick Purnell
P.O. Box 1166 • Cary, NC 27512 • USA
Phone (919) 363-8000
Web site: www.DickPurnell.com

Other excellent Harvest House Books by Dick Purnell

⟡

Finding a Lasting Love

Singles make up 40 percent of the American adult population, and most of them want to find their lifelong mate. Dick Purnell reveals the questions, answers, and insights on dating he shares through conferences, interviews, and articles. Going straight to the heart of the matter, he discusses:

- insights for understanding the opposite sex
- how to avoid short–circuiting a good relationship
- suggestions for finding a potential partner
- what God's Word says about relationships

Finding a Lasting Love is beyond a "how to" for the dating reader. It's a biblical exploration of relationships and an invitation to approach dating and life with a healthy, growing faith. Formerly *Becoming a Friend & Lover*.

Other 31-Day Experiment Bible Studies

Knowing God by His Names

Growing Closer to God